THINKFEST CONSULTING

Introduction

Welcome to the Read-Write-Think Series books for early years to grade 6. In this workbook, we aim to give 7-9 year-olds who are now able to read at elementary level tasks to support their development of mental schemes and to think about parts of those schemes.

Each task gives the child the opportunity to relate a class of objects with a particular word, to name each item in the class and to practice writing out each word.

Even without prior knowledge, each set of four images gives the child chance to make sense of what they see and assess relations between the items. A single or sometimes double letter clue is provided to start off the classification for each task. The next page in each instance is for the child to ask questions of the teacher, guardian or parent of any aspect of the four images that intrigues them. They may be questions about parts of an object, its nature, use, size, uniqueness relative to the others or how it is made.

This workbook will support development of a child's vocabulary, the ability to spell, recognize relationships between pictures and to ask important questions. The back of the workbook has a guide to all the scheme labels.

Enjoy!

Guide to tasks

The following pages contain tasks that involve relating four pictures to a single word to form a scheme.

A mental scheme is a structure we use to represent some aspect of the world around us.

Here is an example.

Will the learner tell that these are all leaves? Can they pose some questions regarding the unique shapes of the leaves or what is common to all of them? Would they be curious as to why some leaves are green and others are a different color?

One for many

Write one word to represent the 4 pictures

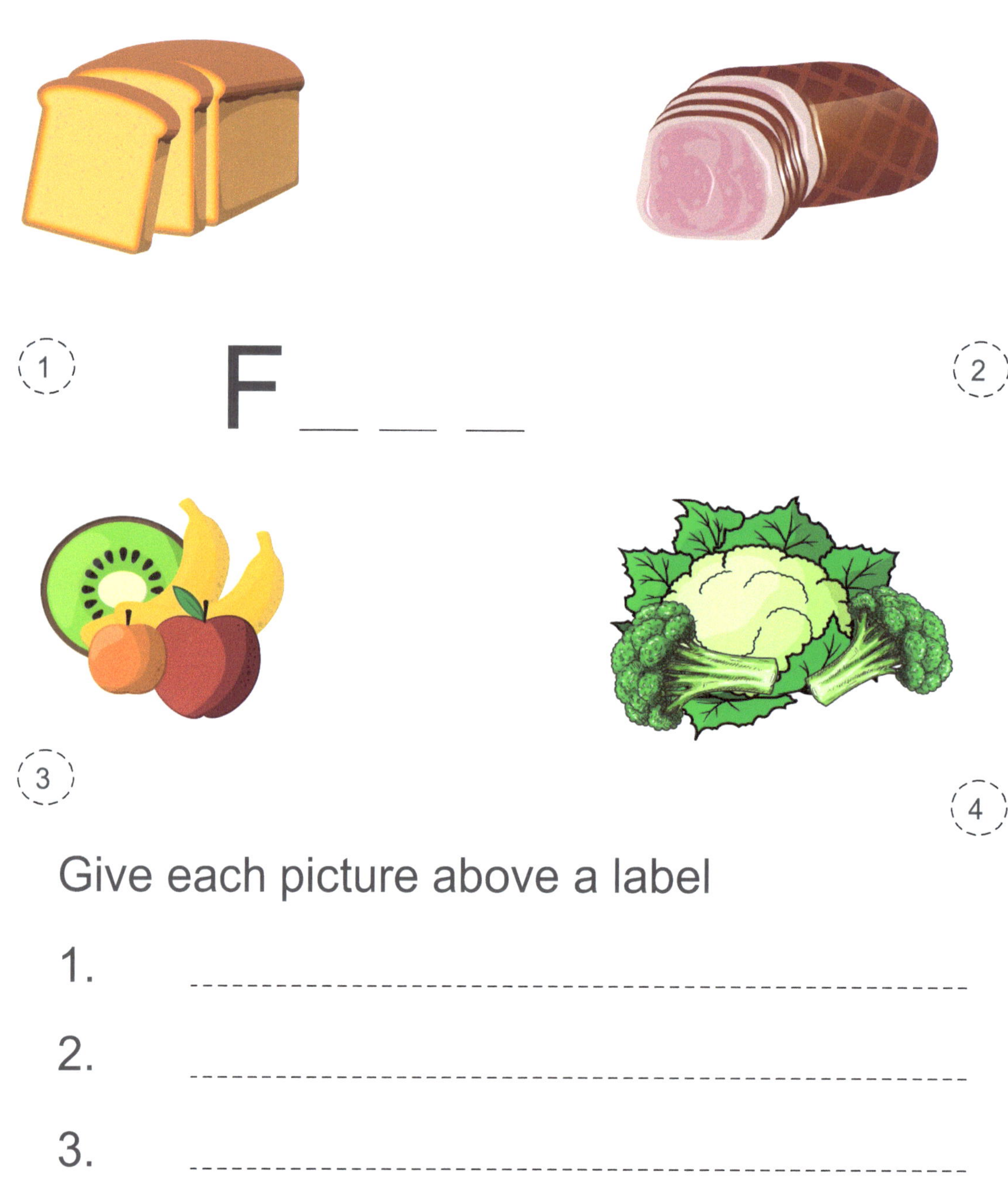

Give each picture above a label

1. --

2. --

3. --

4. --

Are you curious?

Is there something else you would like to know about the items you named and how they are related (why, how, what if)?

Ask a parent/teacher or write your questions here to review later.

One for many

Write one word to represent the 4 pictures

B_ _ _ _ _ _ _ _

3

4

Name (or describe) each picture

1. --

2. --

3. --

4. --

Are you curious?

Is there something else you would like to know about the items you named and how they are related (why, how, what if)?

Ask a parent/teacher or write your questions here to review later.

One for many

Write one word to represent the 4 pictures

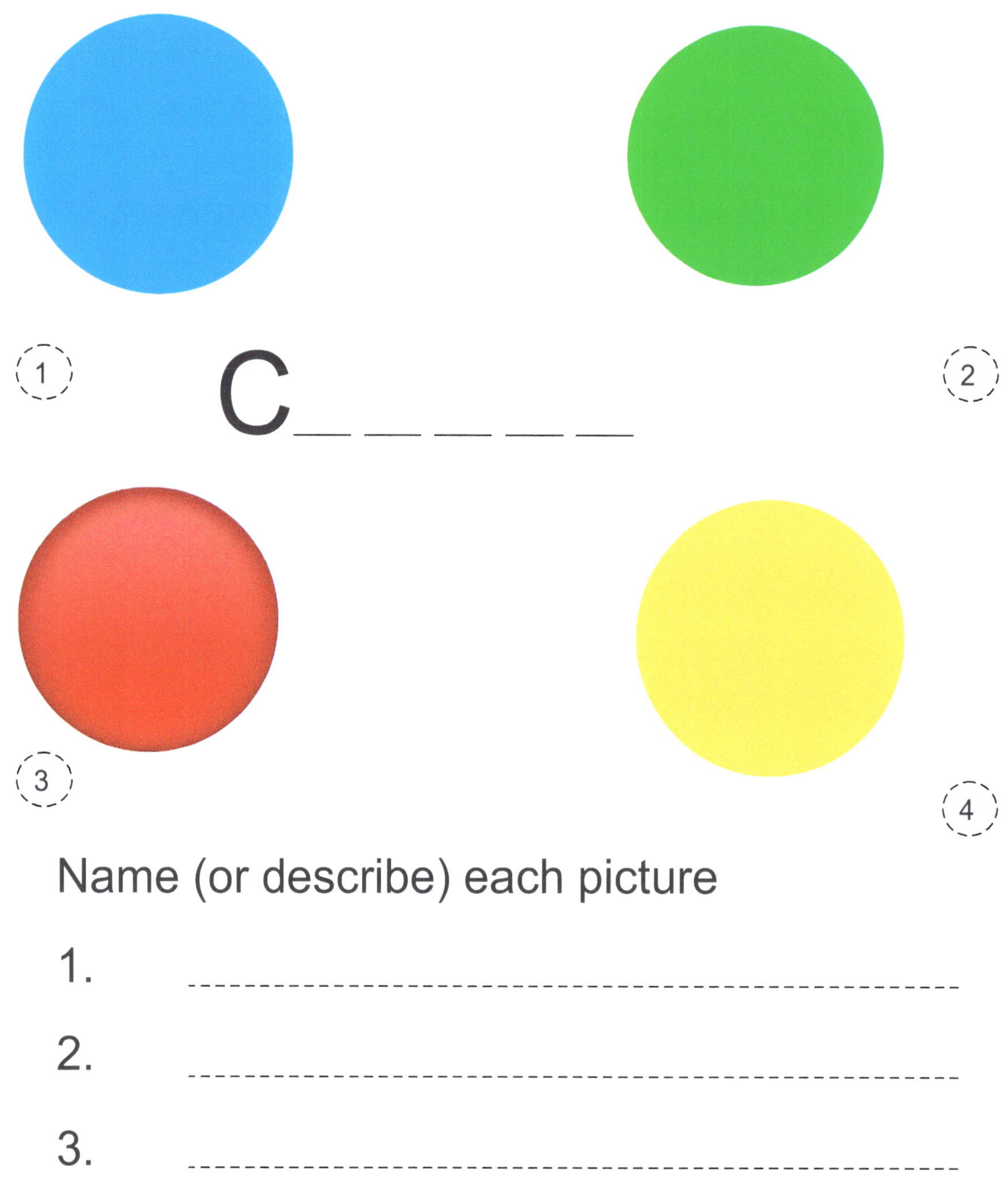

Name (or describe) each picture

1. --
2. --
3. --
4. --

Are you curious?

Is there something else you would like to know about the items you named and how they are related (why, how, what if)?

Ask a parent/teacher or write your questions here to review later.

One for many

Write one word to represent the 4 pictures

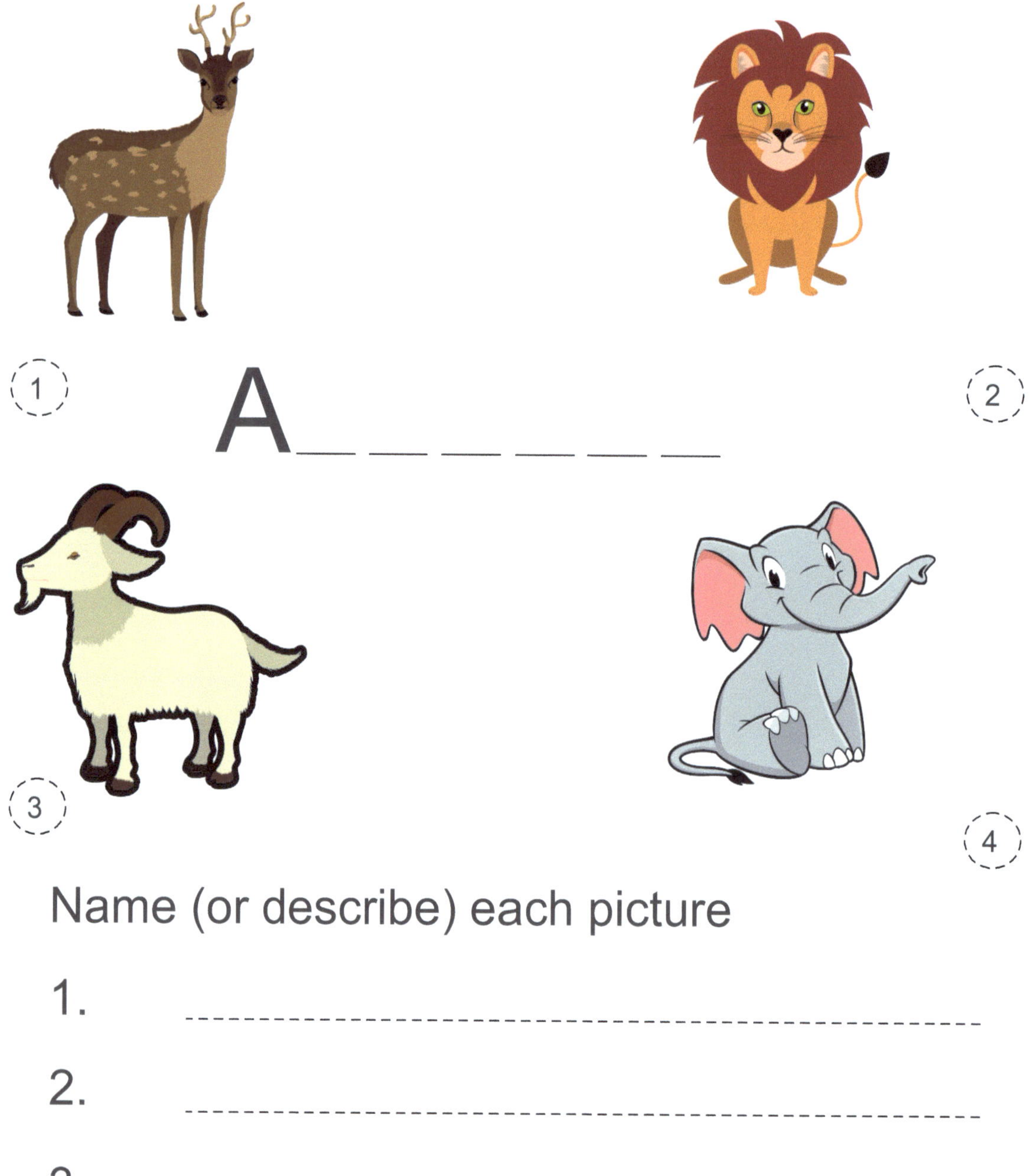

Name (or describe) each picture

1. ______________________________

2. ______________________________

3. ______________________________

4. ______________________________

Are you curious?

Is there something else you would like to know about the items you named and how they are related (why, how, what if)?

Ask a parent/teacher or write your questions here to review later.

One for many

Write one word to represent the 4 pictures

1

F _ _ _ _

3

4

Name (or describe) each picture

1. --

2. --

3. --

4. --

Are you curious?

Is there something else you would like to know about the items you named and how they are related (why, how, what if)?

Ask a parent/teacher or write your questions here to review later.

One for many

Write one word to represent the 4 pictures

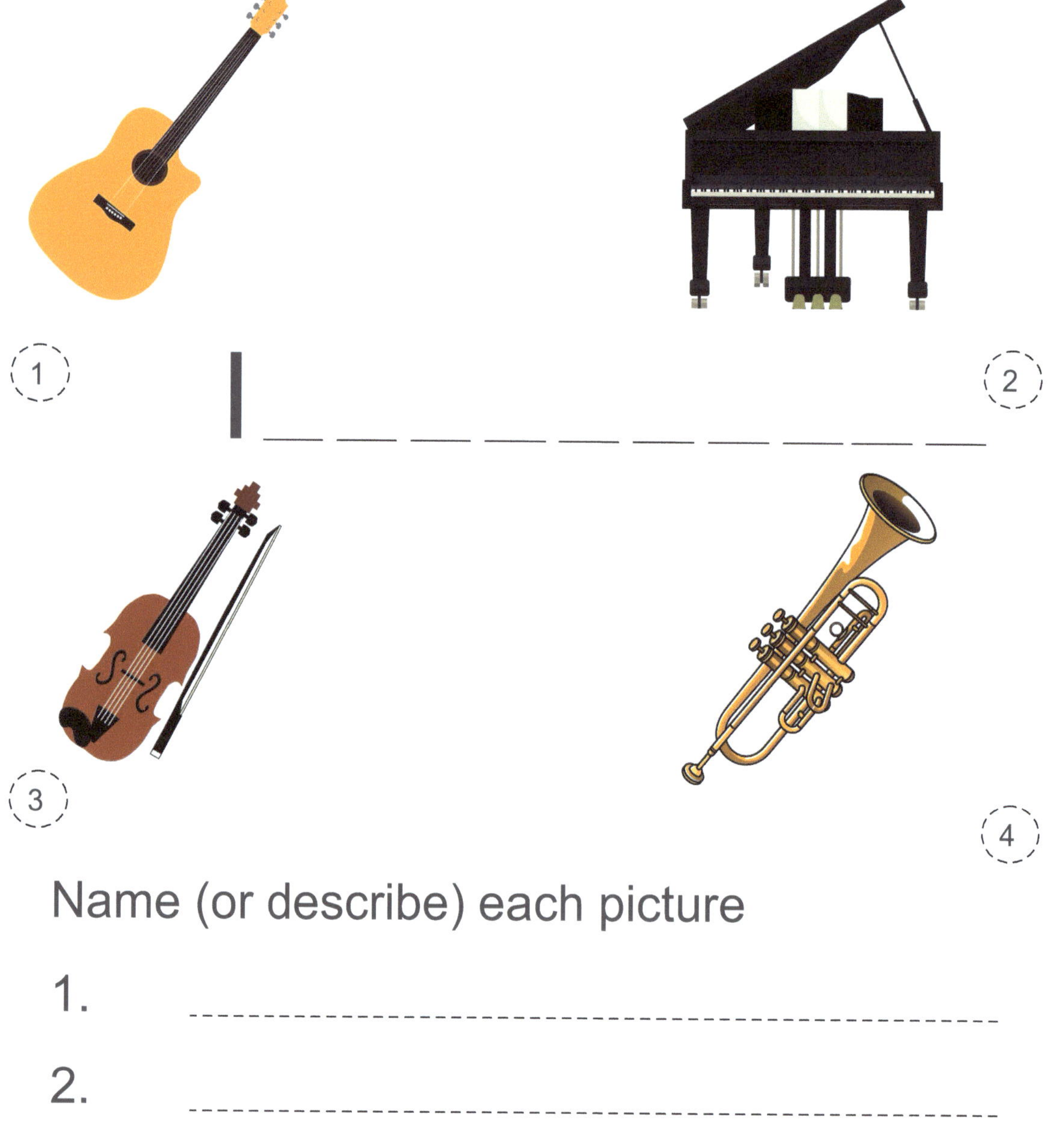

Name (or describe) each picture

1. --

2. --

3. --

4. --

Are you curious?

Is there something else you would like to know about the items you named and how they are related (why, how, what if)?

Ask a parent/teacher or write your questions here to review later.

One for many

Write one word to represent the 4 pictures

1

S_ _ _ _ _

3

4

Name (or describe) each picture

1. --

2. --

3. --

4. --

Are you curious?

Is there something else you would like to know about the items you named and how they are related (why, how, what if)?

Ask a parent/teacher or write your questions here to review later.

One for many

Write one word to represent the 4 pictures

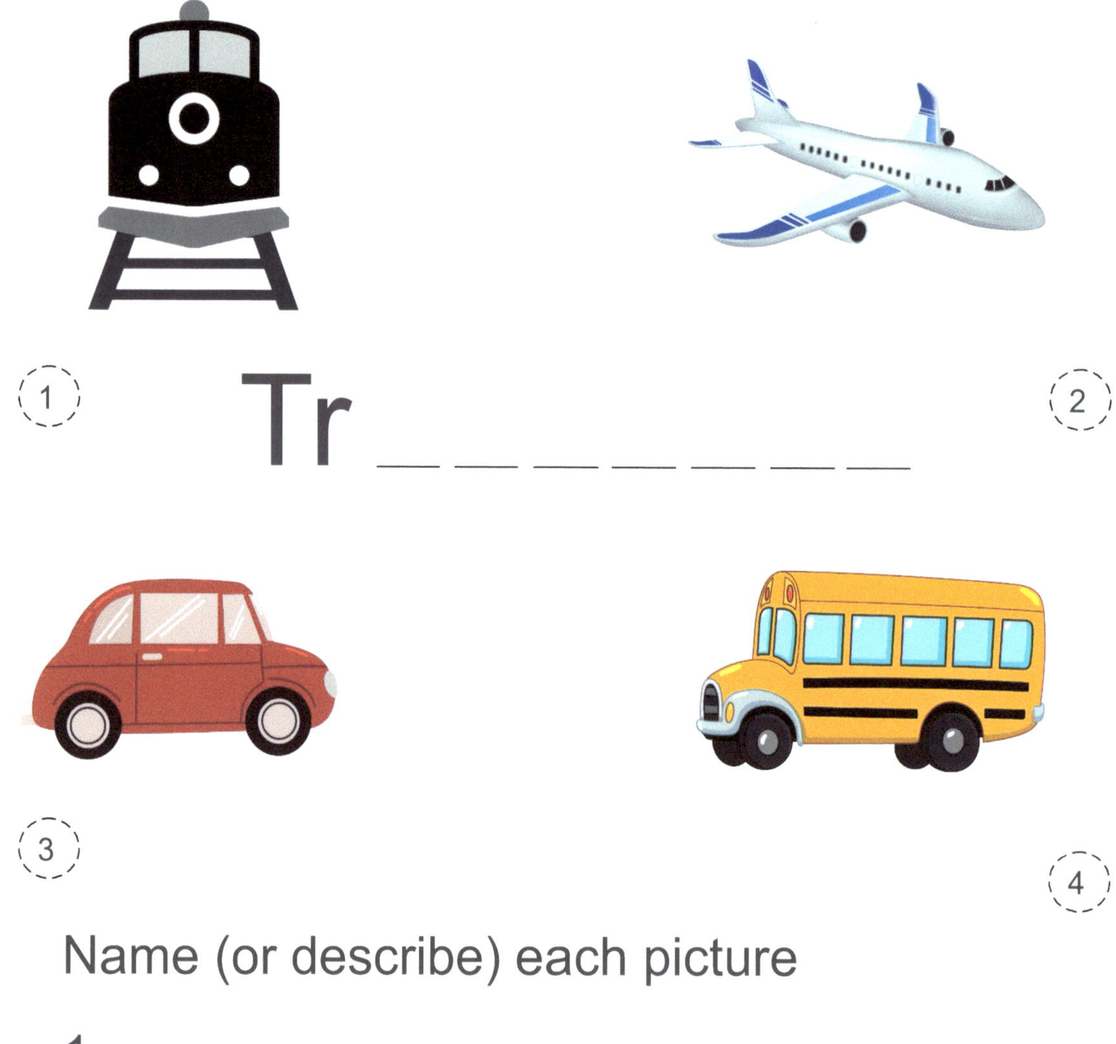

Name (or describe) each picture

1. --

2. --

3. --

4. --

Are you curious?

Is there something else you would like to know about the items you named and how they are related (why, how, what if)?

Ask a parent/teacher or write your questions here to review later.

One for many

Write one word to represent the 4 pictures

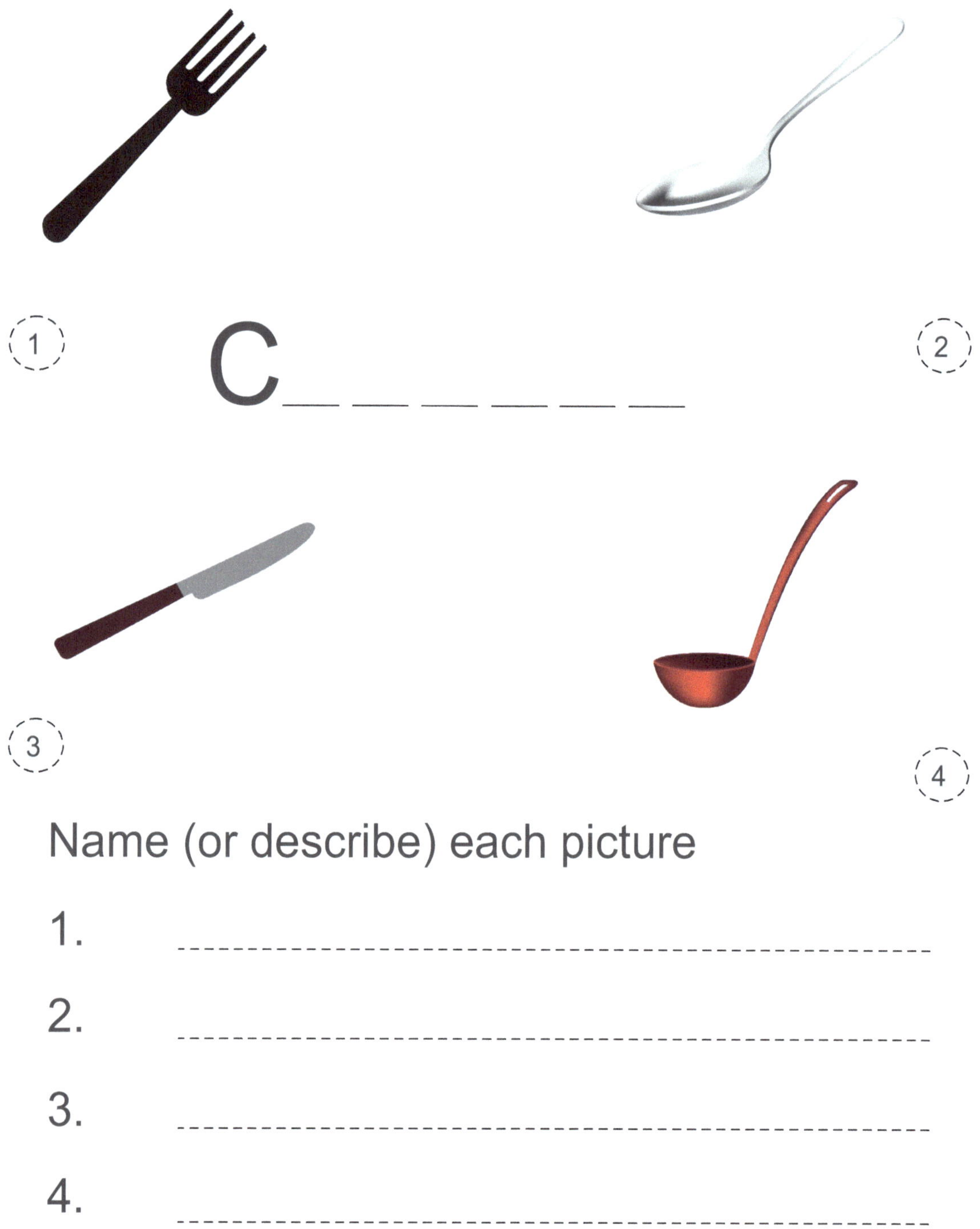

Name (or describe) each picture

1. --

2. --

3. --

4. --

Are you curious?

Is there something else you would like to know about the items you named and how they are related (why, how, what if)?

Ask a parent/teacher or write your questions here to review later.

One for many

Write one word to represent the 4 pictures

1

Co_ _ _ _ _ _ _

2

3

4

Name (or describe) each picture

1. --

2. --

3. --

4. --

Are you curious?

Is there something else you would like to know about the items you named and how they are related (why, how, what if)?

Ask a parent/teacher or write your questions here to review later.

One for many

Write one word to represent the 4 pictures

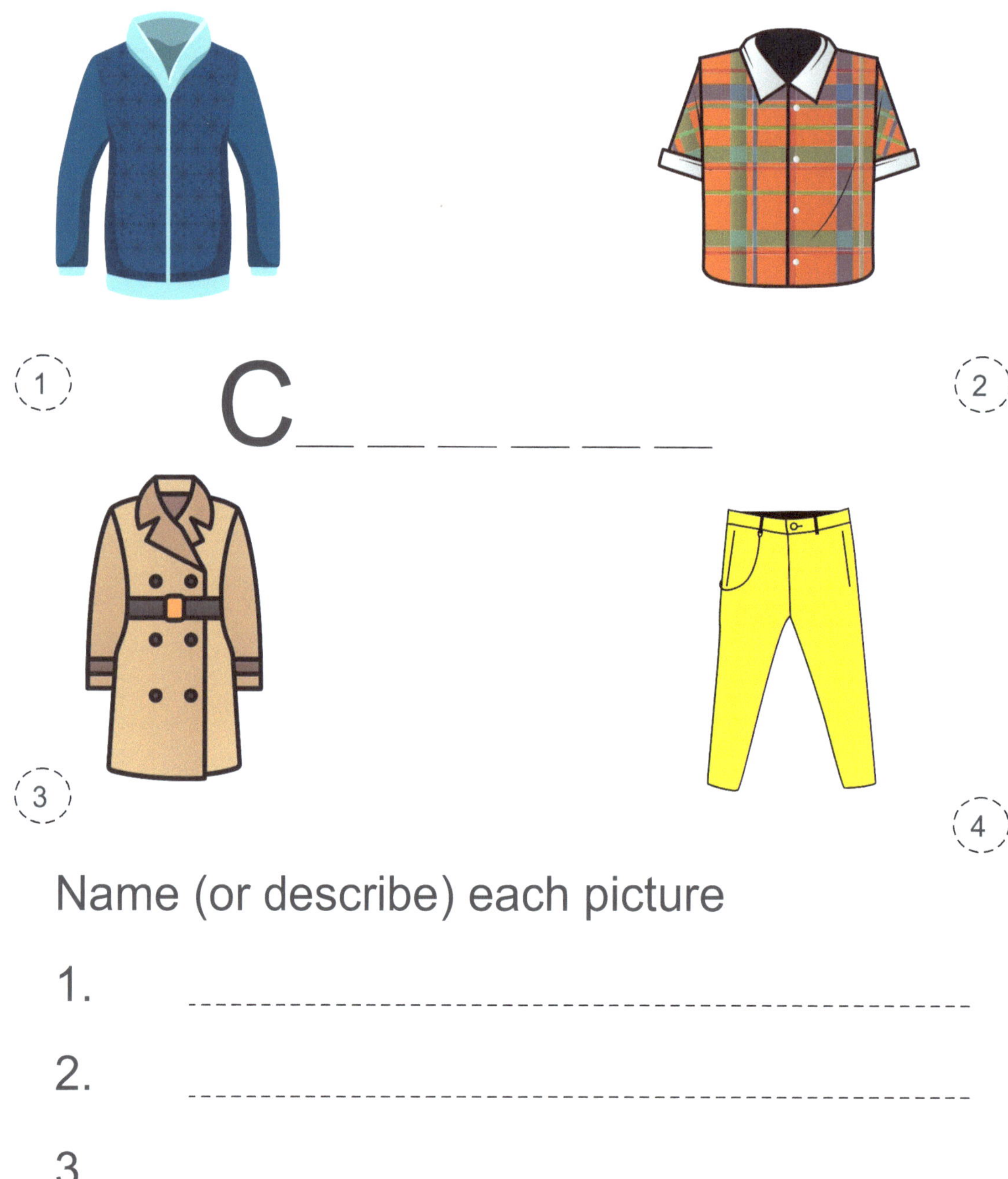

Name (or describe) each picture

1. --

2. --

3. --

4. --

Are you curious?

Is there something else you would like to know about the items you named and how they are related (why, how, what if)?

Ask a parent/teacher or write your questions here to review later.

One for many

Write one word to represent the 4 pictures

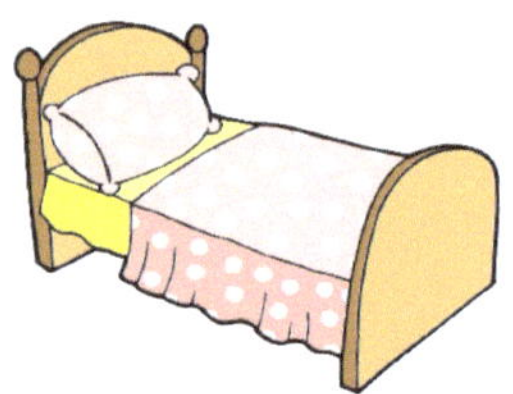

B___ ___ ___

3

4

Name (or describe) each picture

1. --

2. --

3. --

4. --

Are you curious?

Is there something else you would like to know about the items you named and how they are related (why, how, what if)?

Ask a parent/teacher or write your questions here to review later.

One for many

Write one word to represent the 4 pictures

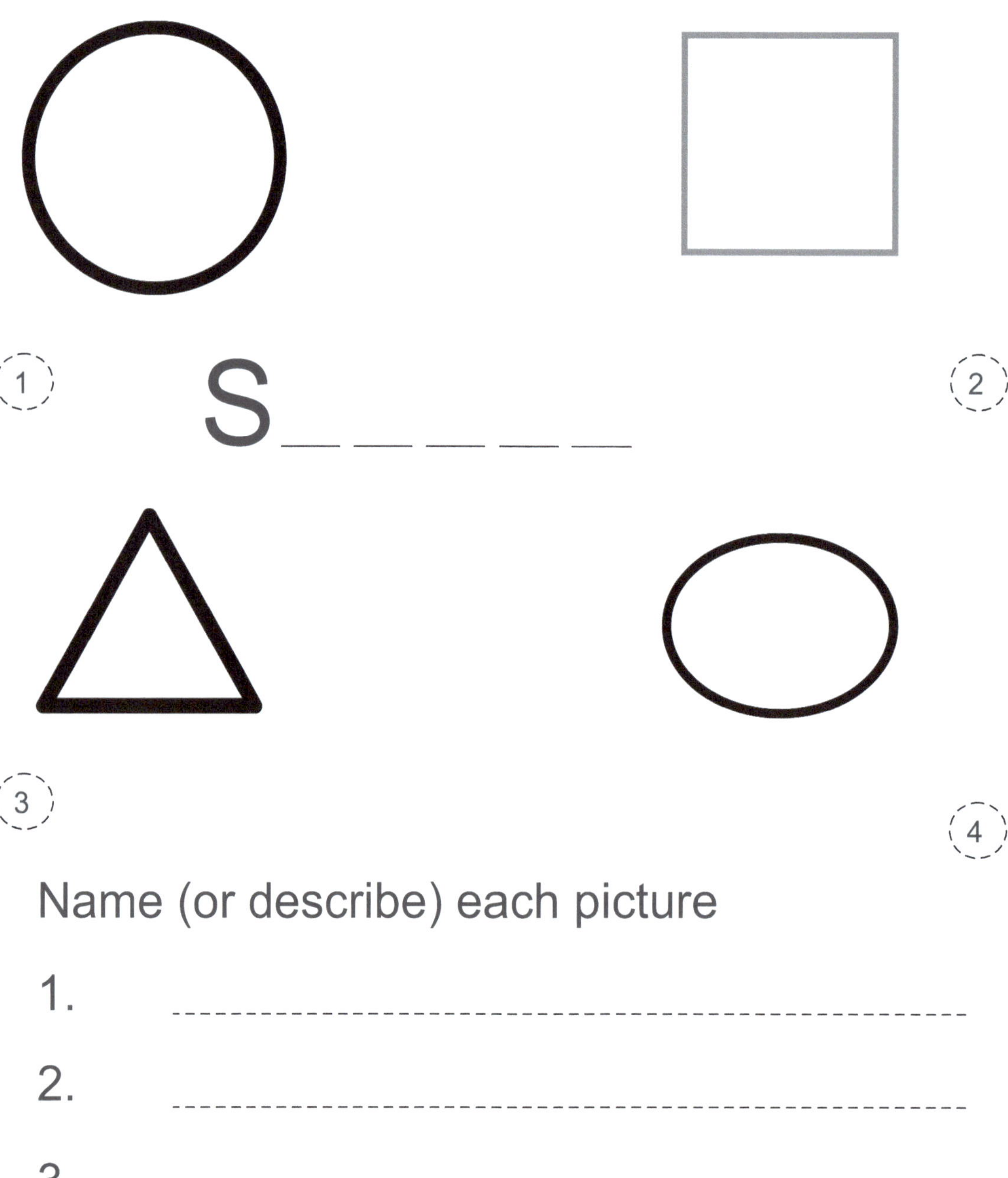

Name (or describe) each picture

1. ....

2. ....

3. ....

4. ....

Are you curious?

Is there something else you would like to know about the items you named and how they are related (why, how, what if)?

Ask a parent/teacher or write your questions here to review later.

One for many

Write one word to represent the 4 pictures

1

S_ _ _ _

3

4

Name (or describe) each picture

1. --

2. --

3. --

4. --

Are you curious?

Is there something else you would like to know about the items you named and how they are related (why, how, what if)?

Ask a parent/teacher or write your questions here to review later.

One for many

Write one word to represent the 4 pictures

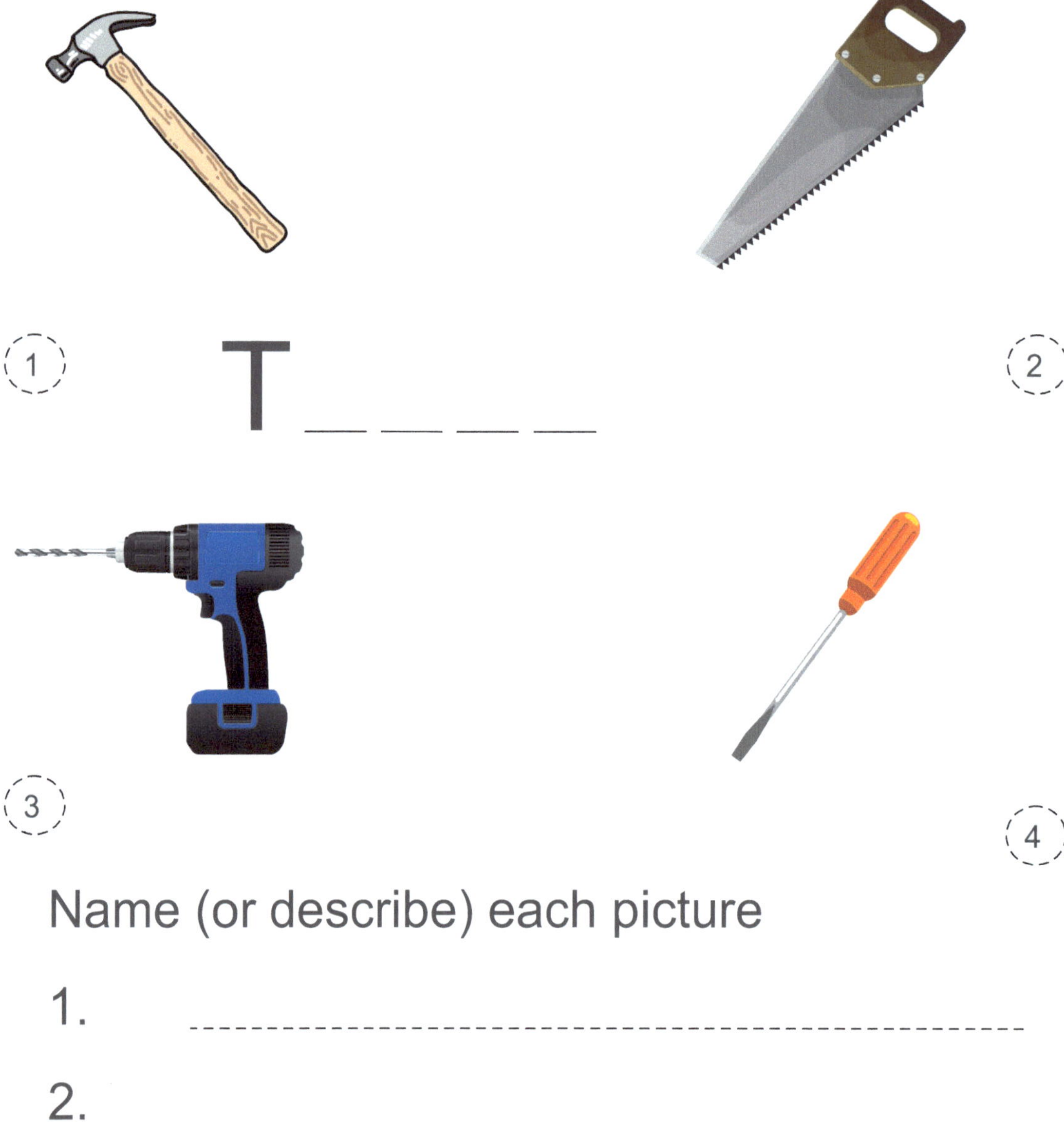

Name (or describe) each picture

1. ______________________________

2. ______________________________

3. ______________________________

4. ______________________________

Are you curious?

Is there something else you would like to know about the items you named and how they are related (why, how, what if)?

Ask a parent/teacher or write your questions here to review later.

One for many

Write one word to represent the 4 pictures

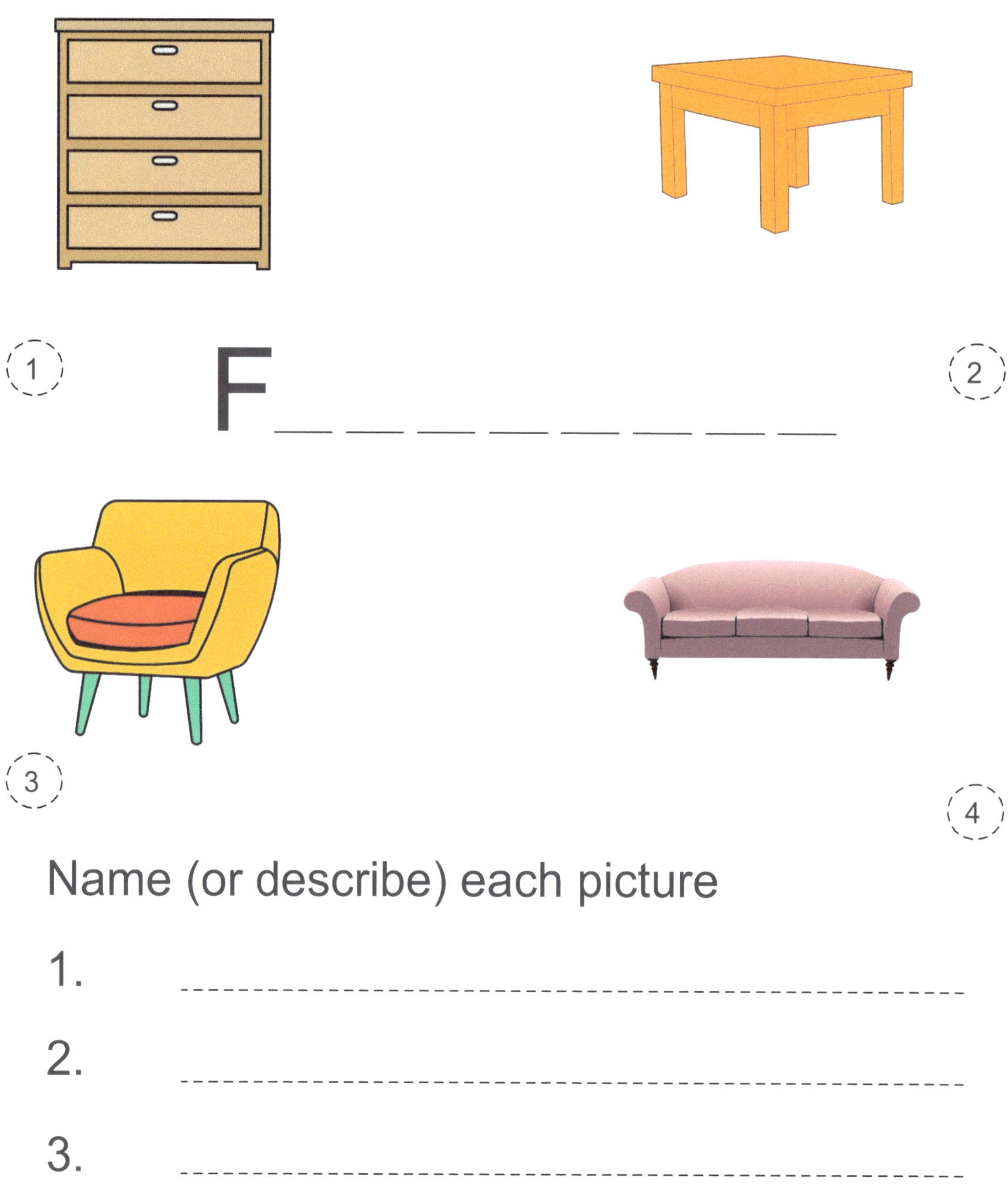

Name (or describe) each picture

1. ______________________

2. ______________________

3. ______________________

4. ______________________

Are you curious?

Is there something else you would like to know about the items you named and how they are related (why, how, what if)?

Ask a parent/teacher or write your questions here to review later.

One for many

Write one word to represent the 4 pictures

1

W_ _ _ _ _

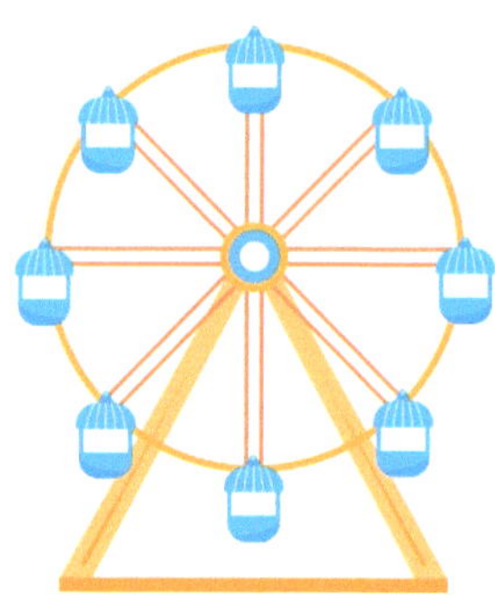

3

4

Name (or describe) each picture

1. --
2. --
3. --
4. --

Are you curious?

Is there something else you would like to know about the items you named and how they are related (why, how, what if)?

Ask a parent/teacher or write your questions here to review later.

One for many

Write one word to represent the 4 pictures

Name (or describe) each picture

1. --
2. --
3. --
4. --

Are you curious?

Is there something else you would like to know about the items you named and how they are related (why, how, what if)?

Ask a parent/teacher or write your questions here to review later.

One for many

Write one word to represent the 4 pictures

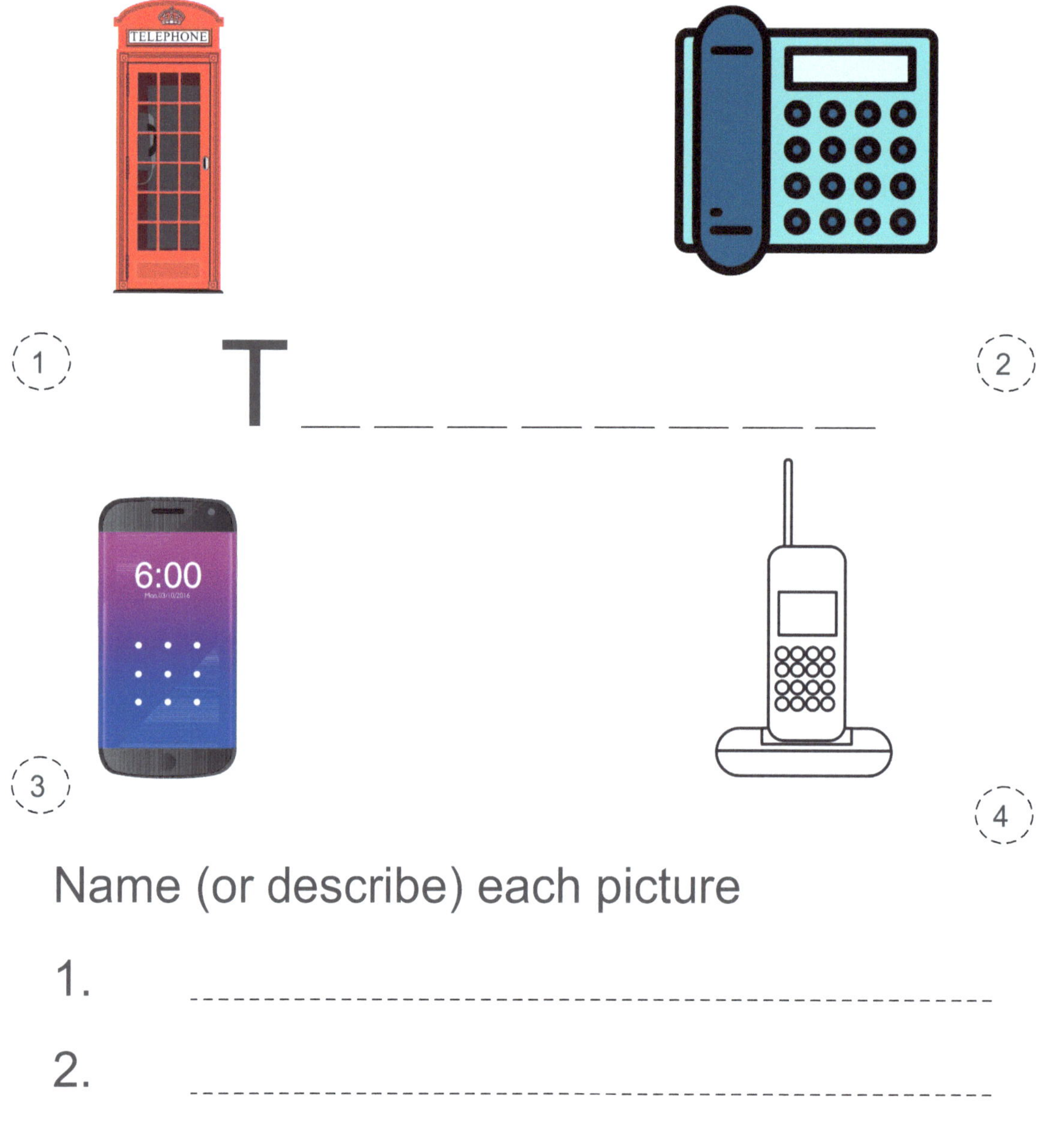

Name (or describe) each picture

1. ....

2. ....

3. ....

4. ....

Are you curious?

Is there something else you would like to know about the items you named and how they are related (why, how, what if)?

Ask a parent/teacher or write your questions here to review later.

One for many

Write one word to represent the 4 pictures

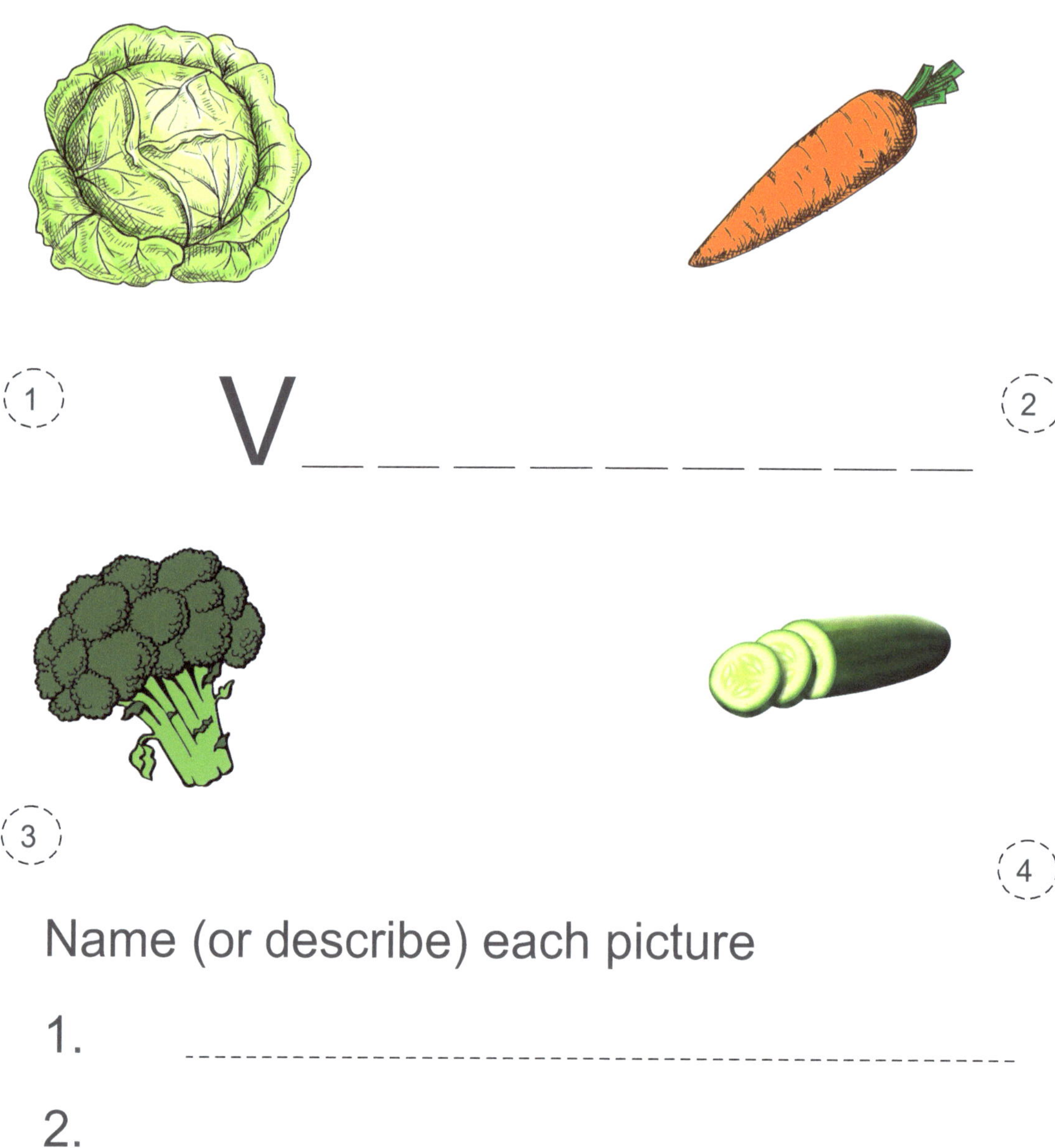

Name (or describe) each picture

1. ______________________

2. ______________________

3. ______________________

4. ______________________

Are you curious?

Is there something else you would like to know about the items you named and how they are related (why, how, what if)?

Ask a parent/teacher or write your questions here to review later.

One for many

Write one word to represent the 4 pictures

1

S_ _ _ _

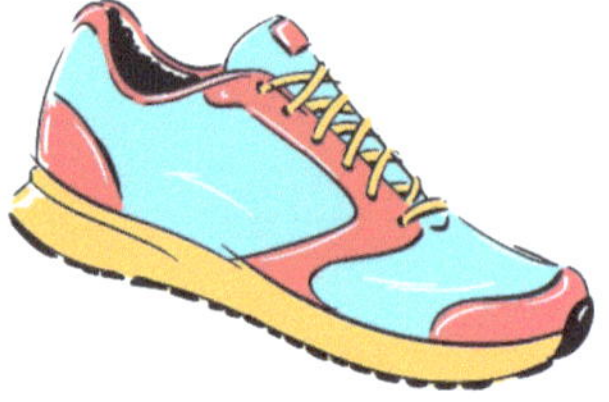

3

4

Name (or describe) each picture

1. --

2. --

3. --

4. --

Are you curious?

Is there something else you would like to know about the items you named and how they are related (why, how, what if)?

Ask a parent/teacher or write your questions here to review later.

One for many

Write one word to represent the 4 pictures

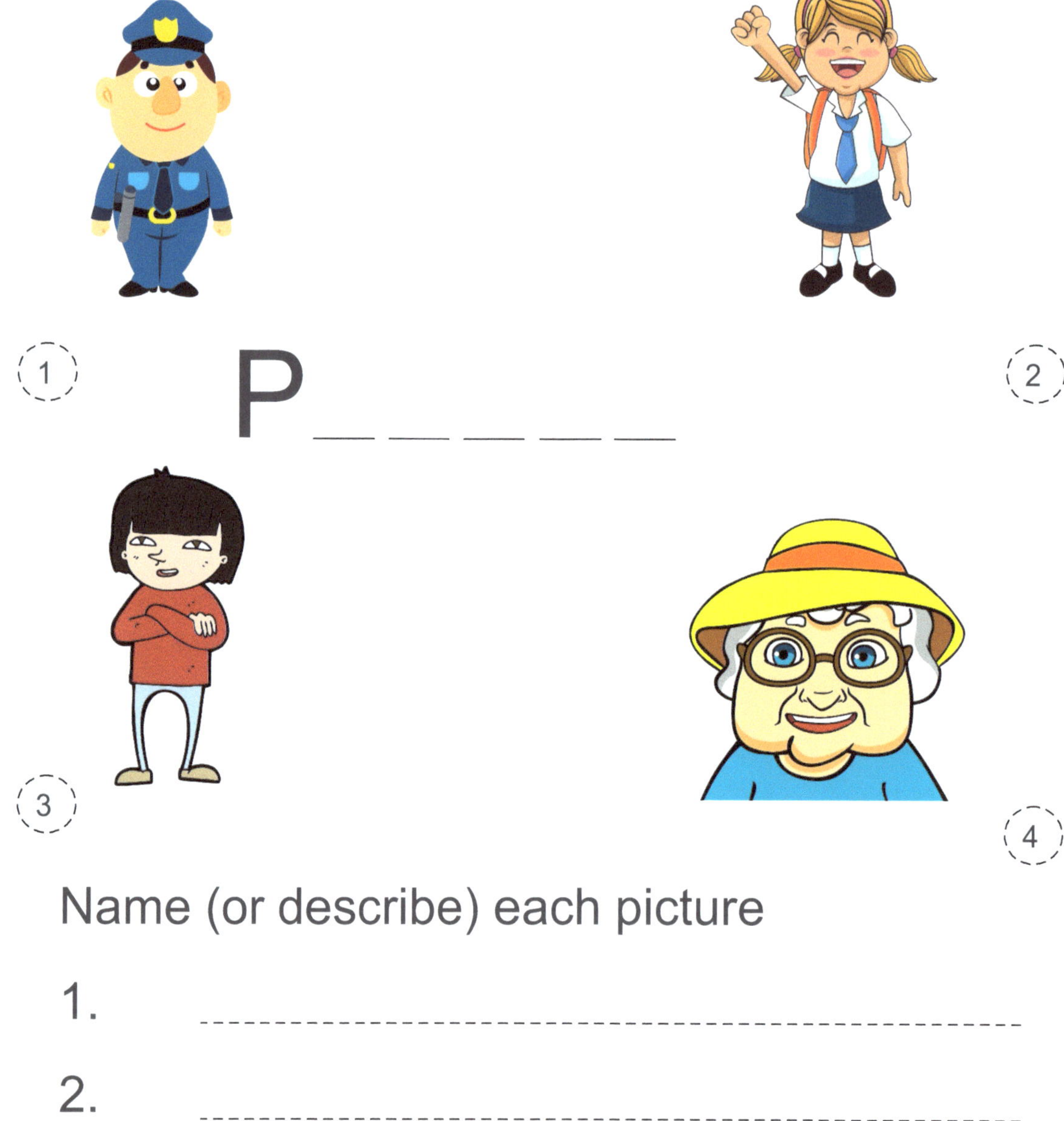

Name (or describe) each picture

1. ______________________

2. ______________________

3. ______________________

4. ______________________

Are you curious?

Is there something else you would like to know about the items you named and how they are related (why, how, what if)?

Ask a parent/teacher or write your questions here to review later.

Picture descriptions

Pg. 6 Food (bread, ham, fruit, vegetables)

Pg. 8 Buildings (house, skyscraper, school, church)

Pg. 10 Colors (blue, green, read and yellow)

Pg. 12 Animals (deer, lion, goat and elephant)

Pg. 14 Fruit (grapes, orange, strawberry and pear)

Pg. 16 Instruments (guitar, piano, violin and trumpet)

Pg. 18 Sports (tennis, basketball, football, hockey)

Pg. 20 Transport (train, airplane, car and bus)

Pg. 22 Cutlery (fork, spoon, knife and ladle)

Pg. 24 Containers (water bottle, milk container, bottle, garbage can)

Pg. 26 Clothes (Sweater, short, coat and pants)

Pg. 28 Beds (Baby bed or bed, bunk bed, hospital bed, crib)

Pg. 30 Shapes (Circle, square, triangle and oval)

Pg. 32 Signs (Stop, direction, no pets and no photos)

www.ingramcontent.com/pod-product-compliance
Ingram Content Group UK Ltd.
Pitfield, Milton Keynes, MK11 3LW, UK
UKHW060104300726
14090UKWH00003B/372

* 9 7 8 1 9 9 9 0 8 3 6 6 3 *